Conditional love imprisons you, unconditional love liberates you.

Dear Adele,
   this book is a special gift for you!
      With warmest
         love
         &
      blessings
      Ratanjit
      10/16/19

101 Gems for Re-Aligning Your Life

Ratanjit
RATANJIT S. SONDHE

Copyright © 2017 Ratanjit S. Sondhe.

All rights reserved. No part of this book may be used or reproduced by any means, graphic, electronic, or mechanical, including photocopying, recording, taping or by any information storage retrieval system without the written permission of the author except in the case of brief quotations embodied in critical articles and reviews.

This book is a work of non-fiction. Unless otherwise noted, the author and the publisher make no explicit guarantees as to the accuracy of the information contained in this book and in some cases, names of people and places have been altered to protect their privacy.

Balboa Press books may be ordered through booksellers or by contacting:

Balboa Press
A Division of Hay House
1663 Liberty Drive
Bloomington, IN 47403
www.balboapress.com
1 (877) 407-4847

Because of the dynamic nature of the Internet, any web addresses or links contained in this book may have changed since publication and may no longer be valid. The views expressed in this work are solely those of the author and do not necessarily reflect the views of the publisher, and the publisher hereby disclaims any responsibility for them.

Interior book design: David Christel

Any people depicted in stock imagery provided by Thinkstock are models, and such images are being used for illustrative purposes only.
Certain stock imagery © Thinkstock.

ISBN: 978-1-5043-3784-7 (hc)

Library of Congress Control Number: 2016914282

Printed in the United States.

Balboa Press rev. date: 03/08/2017

Dedication

This book is dedicated to the power and majesty of the bigger ONE in you and within all of us.

Other Books by Ratanjit

How Oneness Changes Everything
Empowering Business Through 9 Universal Laws

TEA: The Recipe for Stress-Free Living

The Secret of Our Ultimate Success

Audios & Videos

The 9 Universal Laws of Success

The 25 Habits for Success

Introduction

In a world sorely lacking in compassion, grace, depth and respectful regard for one another, truth and clarity of purpose are hard to come by. Life offers innumerable distractions and diverting experiences that challenge us to remain centered in our hearts. We forget that we are an integral component of Nature, interconnected with all of humanity and that we have the ability to create a world very different from that we currently know.

In essence, we have forgotten who we truly are, what our ultimate purpose in life is and why our every thought, word, and action carries the seeds of illumination and true freedom to be shared unconditionally with all of humankind.

In spite of our noblest intentions, highest education, best technology, maximum efforts and total commitment of all our resources, we will fail to make this world a better place if the timeless truth of Oneness is not understood and implemented in each and every aspect of our thinking and living.

The quotes in this book are in themselves, contemplations of the truth of Oneness. Allow them to gently rest within your inner being, be lightly borne through your consciousness as you approach each day, every circumstance, every relationship. They are my Divine gift to you to be shared with the rest of the world from my heart to yours to the heart of all life.

Ratanjit

101 Gems for Re-Aligning Your Life

The only absolute truth...

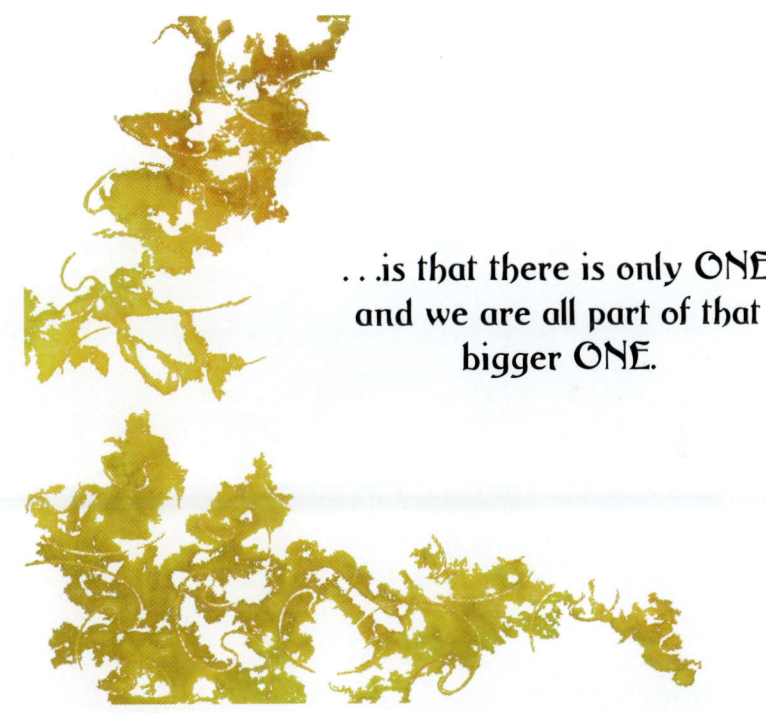

...is that there is only ONE and we are all part of that bigger ONE.

All questions originate in the mind...

~ But the true answers always reside in the heart.

Education is only a tool...

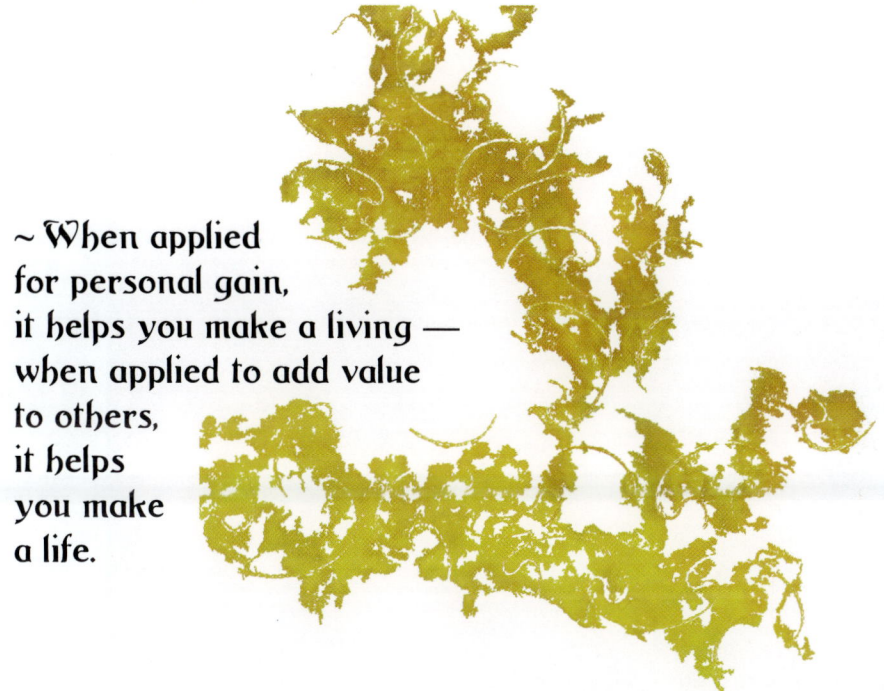

~ When applied
for personal gain,
it helps you make a living —
when applied to add value
to others,
it helps
you make
a life.

What you see, experience, and know...

...remains incomplete and erroneous
    until you unveil the timeless truth
                within yourself.

Our unconditional and continuous gratefulness for the gift of life...

...will empower us to change every hurdle into an award-winning trophy.

Gratefulness for the gift of life that is unconditional and continuous changes every hurdle into victory.

Education, talent, intelligence, experience, and money are just resources allocated to us and not owned by us...

~ When used to add value unconditionally, we achieve true success and a stress-free life.

When used selfishly without adding value to others, even our successes become failures and our lives stress filled.

An ownership mindset causes a tremendous amount of stress...

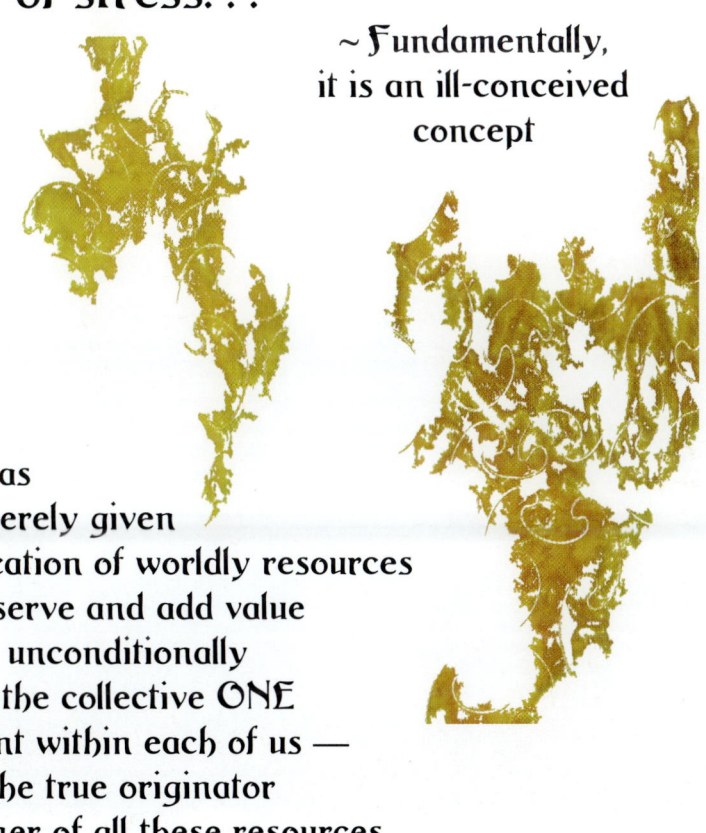

~ Fundamentally, it is an ill-conceived concept

as
we are merely given
an allocation of worldly resources
to serve and add value
unconditionally
to the collective ONE
present within each of us —
the true originator
and owner of all these resources.

Boredom is simply an indicator that you're not focusing on your true passion...

~ You can't find
your true passion
until you discover
the real purpose
of your life,
which only becomes clear
when you know who you really are.

To gain empowering self-respect and dignity, you must take on a mission of truly serving unconditionally…

~ To instill this, develop a mindset of selflessly adding the highest value in every thought, act, and encounter. To sustain this path, maintain a constant attitude of utter gratefulness and always remain in student mode.

We do not see things as they really are...

~ That is why we can't see the true self within us because all of our realities are tainted by our egos, fear, greed, insecurities, and personal agendas.

All our insecurities, worries, pains, stresses, fears, etc., are brought about by our

quintessential "ego"...

~ Our ego is merely the absence of the fundamental Truth of Oneness. In the absence of this Truth, we see ourselves as a separate entity rather than an integral part of the omnipresent ONE.

All good deeds done with conditions and expectations only create stress and disappointment...

~ To live stress free, focus on serving unconditionally by adding the highest value in every encounter and opportunity. This process will heal you and provide unlimited, creative fuel for life itself.

We simply can never be ethical until we practice Oneness in every thought and action...

~ When we cheat others and cause them pain, we are in fact causing self-agony and stress. A seed of fundamental ethical thinking is planted when we realize we are all intrinsically connected as ONE and can't cheat others without cheating ourselves.

All of our inner strength and balance comes from being truthful...

~ You cannot be truthful
until you realize,
understand , and live the truth
of Oneness.

That truth inspires you
to make a difference
to others and sets you
on a path of
continuous success.

Self-assurance comes from living in the Oneness paradigm, which leads to self-awareness...

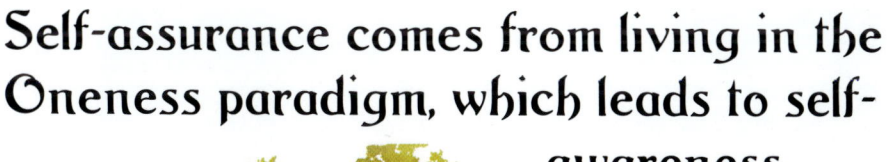

~ Operating as a separate entity produces self-doubt and insecurity, which only supports our egos and creates conflict in all areas of our lives.

We expose more of who we truly are by the questions we ask rather than by the answers we give...

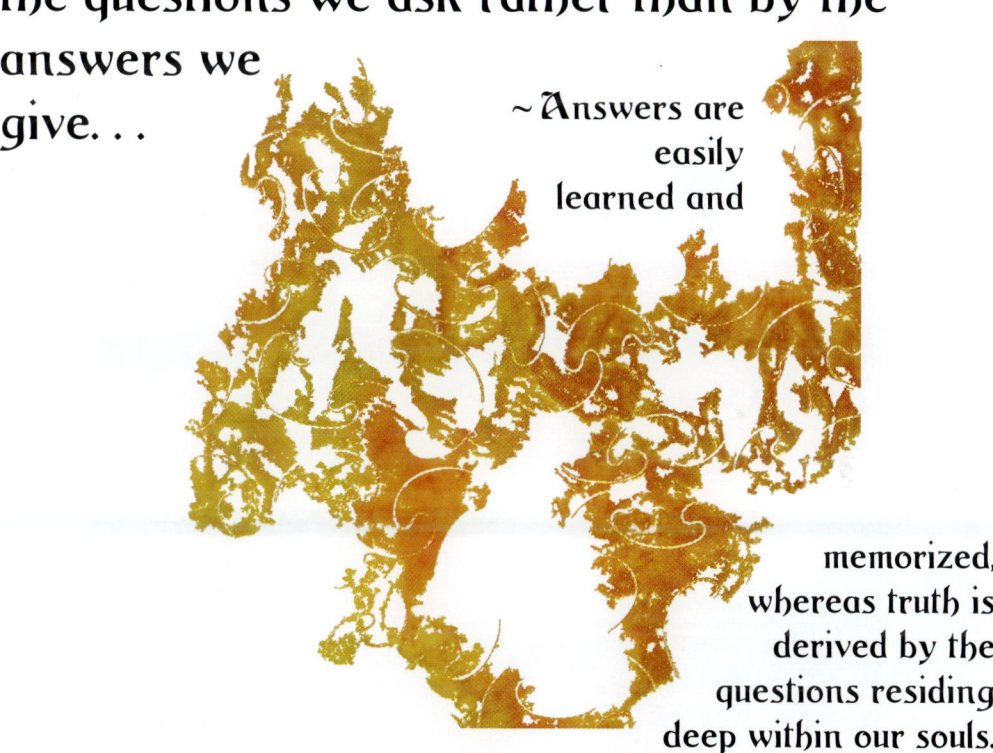

~ Answers are easily learned and memorized, whereas truth is derived by the questions residing deep within our souls.

Our true character is shaped by the fundamental and essential questions planted within our hearts — where the Divine resides...

~ Rather than the erroneous information and knowledge manipulated by our minds and egos.

Passion is never hidden in a subject, talent, or know-how...

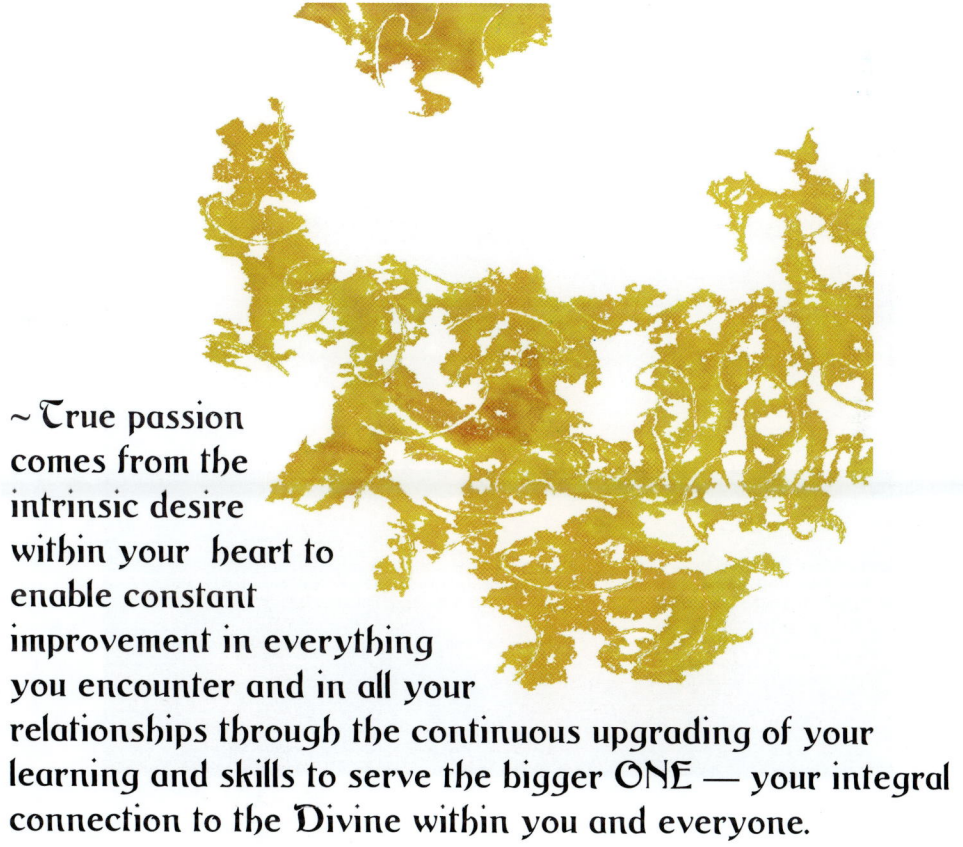

~ True passion comes from the intrinsic desire within your heart to enable constant improvement in everything you encounter and in all your relationships through the continuous upgrading of your learning and skills to serve the bigger ONE — your integral connection to the Divine within you and everyone.

Nature has designed you as an original masterpiece...

~ Take time to unveil your true self first as that will reveal your central purpose in life and thus, your greatest passion, which will set you free and position you to reach your pinnacle of real and lasting success.

A purpose-filled life doesn't have room for self-pity or depression...

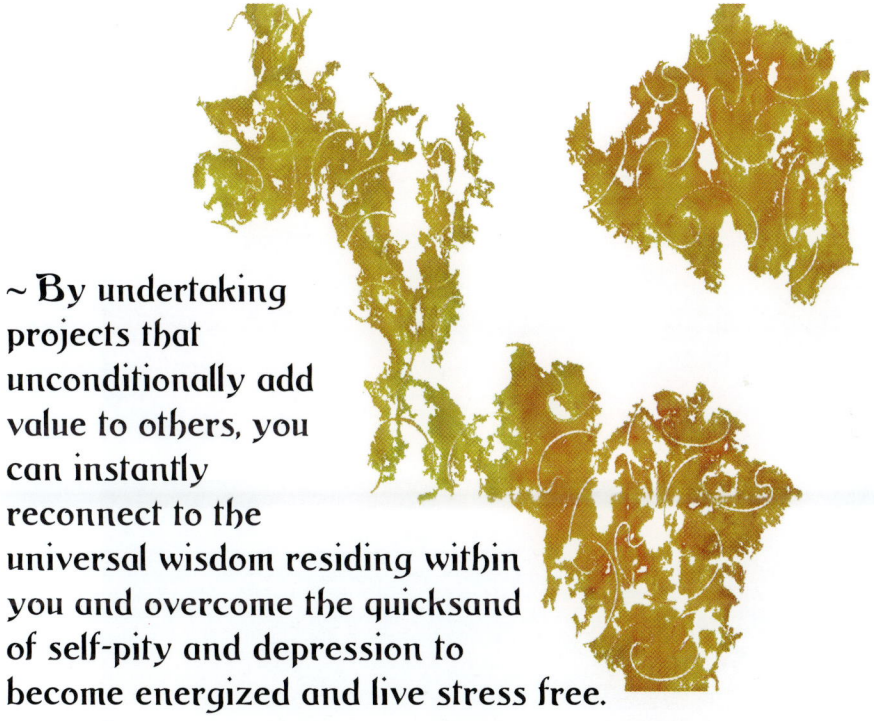

~ By undertaking projects that unconditionally add value to others, you can instantly reconnect to the universal wisdom residing within you and overcome the quicksand of self-pity and depression to become energized and live stress free.

The intrinsic goodness in you is pure Divinity...

~ Once you can see
the goodness in yourself,
you can see
the goodness —
and thus the Divine —
in others. Divinity can never
be owned or demanded.
It can only be recognized,
admired, saluted,
and served.

Difficulties are presented by nature's school of wisdom to teach you the true meaning of life...

~ It challenges you to unveil the true you — the Divine power in you that is free of worldly pain and suffering — and at the same time empowers you to understand and unconditionally serve the pain and suffering in others.

The measure of our true success...

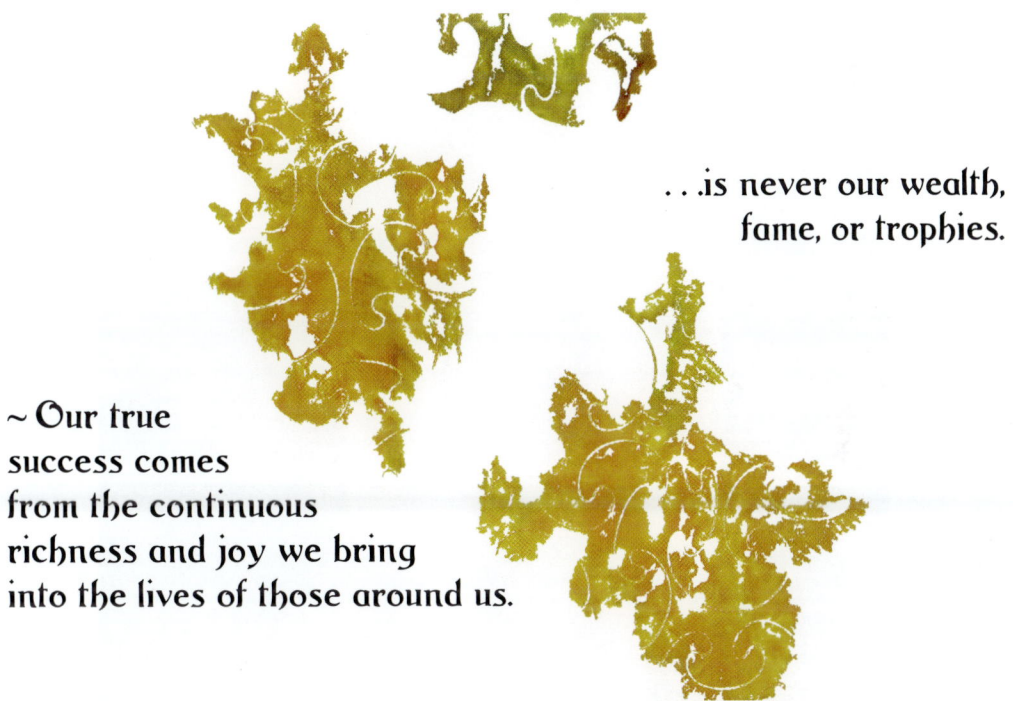

...is never our wealth, fame, or trophies.

~ Our true success comes from the continuous richness and joy we bring into the lives of those around us.

Selflessness inspires us to attain a mindset of uninhibited and random

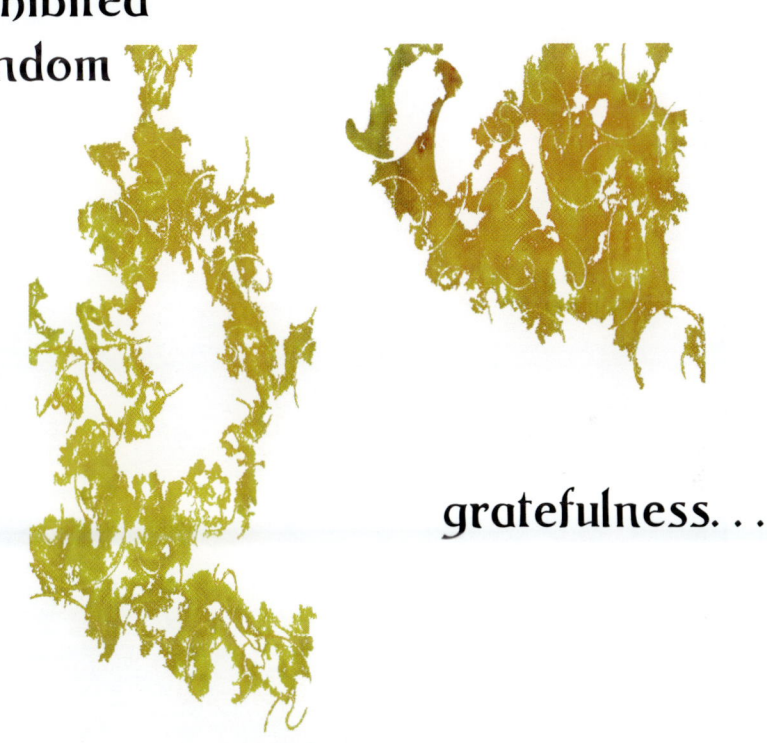

gratefulness...

...which is essential
for stress-free and productive living.

Your best guide or coach resides right within you…

~ To avail yourself of it, simply stay clear of fear, greed, prejudice, ego, jealousy, and selfish agendas while remaining immersed in utter gratefulness.

It is only when you begin to see One in all and all in One that your life will fall into place...

~ You will be judgmental, afraid, stressed, and confused until you remove the illusion of duality within you. You will then experience perfect peace, harmony, and true progress in every aspect of your life.

Religion makes you believe in God — spirituality makes you see and feel God...

~ To see and feel God, look for and serve God in everyone you come across including your own self.

The presence of duality means the absence of spirituality...

~ When we separate our personal life from our professional life, we create duality because the real purpose of our lives is to add the highest value to the ONE in all —
at all times.

The world will judge you from your past performance...

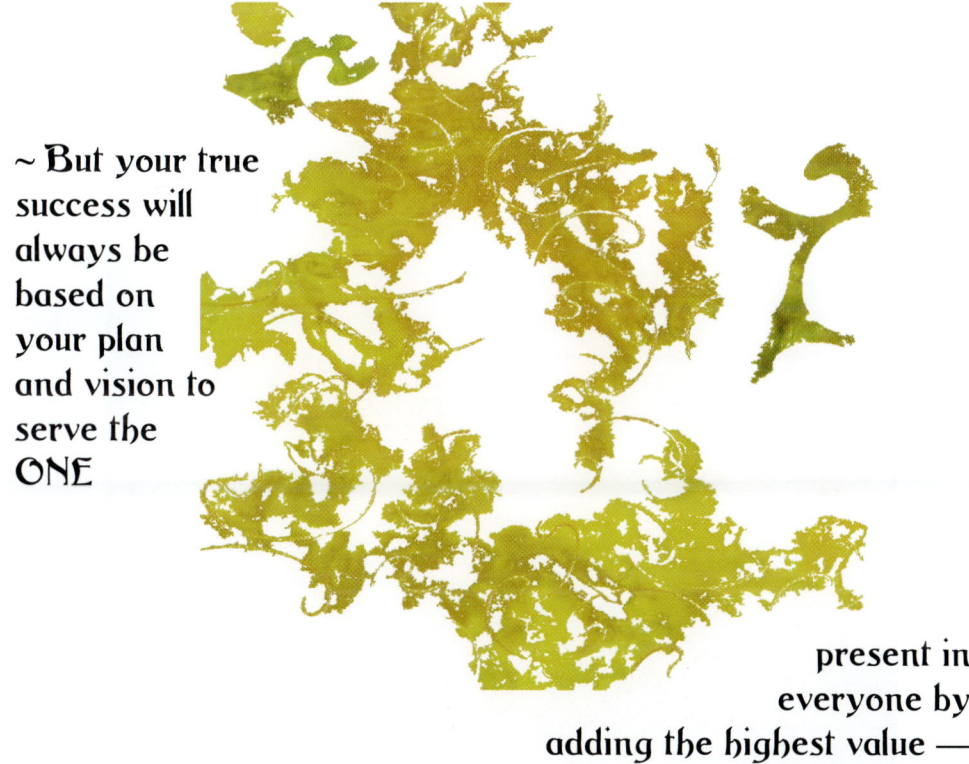

~ But your true success will always be based on your plan and vision to serve the ONE

present in everyone by adding the highest value — unconditionally.

Until we find our true anchor, we will be aimlessly drifting all our lives chasing falsehoods and illusions...

~ It is our connection to the Divine power already planted within us that gives us our anchor

and guides us in a purpose-filled life resulting in lasting peace, joy, and harmony.

Love and respect are the most important factors in effective communication...

~ We may speak the most sophisticated language containing highly relevant material, but until our tone and body language reflect unconditional love and respect, we will always be misunderstood and perplexed.

The joy of doing a task becomes elevated if you simply focus on doing your best without any conditions or expectations...

~ This thought process is in complete alignment with the Divine wisdom within you. That's why you remain stress free despite working hard.

Serving Oneness unconditionally within yourself and others requires continuously exploring and conquering new horizons...

~ However, to climb a new peak, you must leave behind all of your trophies, medals, and extra baggage collected from your earlier successes as they are merely feeding your ego, which will always hold you back.

Life is less about winning and more about not accepting failures...

~ We only accept failures when we see ourselves as being alone or our resources depleted and limited. In reality, we are always a part of the bigger ONE, which gives us unlimited resources — provided our mission is unconditionally adding the highest value in all our endeavors.

The quality of your relationships is always centered around the true you, which is free of ego...

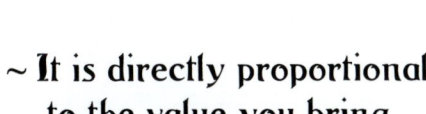

~ It is directly proportional to the value you bring to any relationship.

That is why you cannot have a spouse, you can only be a spouse. You cannot have a friend, you can only be a friend. You cannot have a child, you can only be a parent. You cannot be a boss, you can only be a servant.

Giving with an expectation is not only unethical, but like making a commitment for others without their consent...

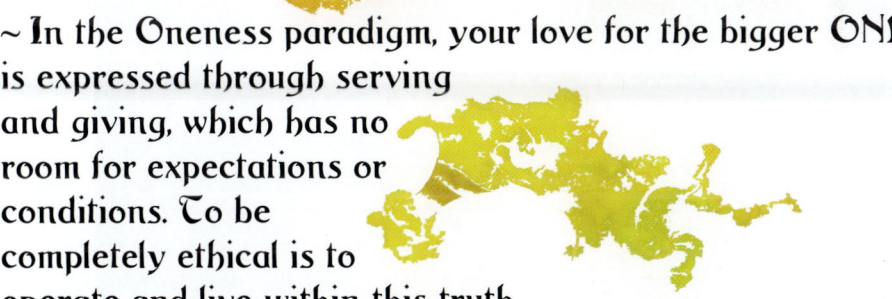

~ In the Oneness paradigm, your love for the bigger ONE is expressed through serving and giving, which has no room for expectations or conditions. To be completely ethical is to operate and live within this truth.

True confidence comes from knowing and connecting to the Divinity within you...

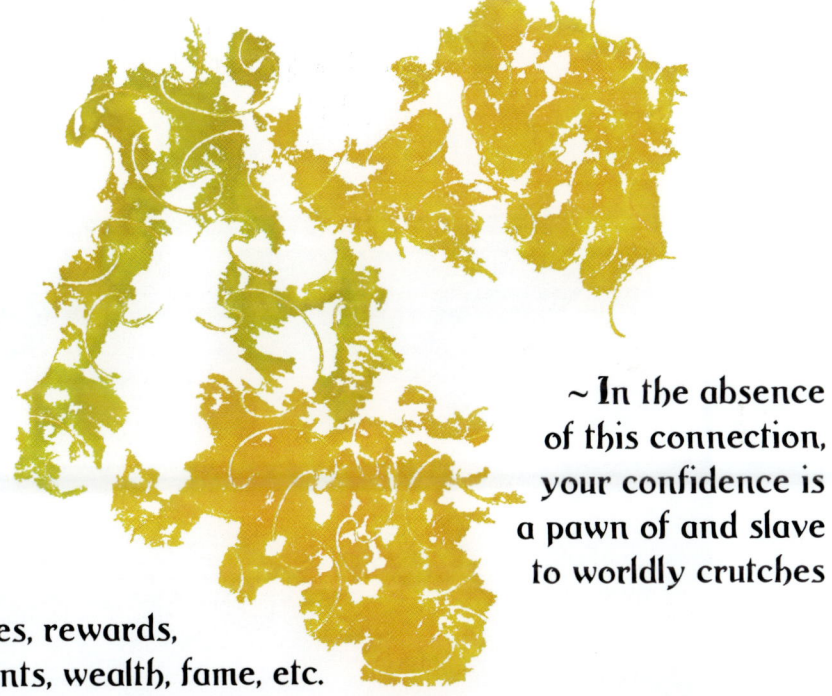

~ In the absence of this connection, your confidence is a pawn of and slave to worldly crutches such as titles, rewards, endorsements, wealth, fame, etc.

Your connection to the Divine within you will enhance your true self-worth by focusing you on a path of serving the bigger ONE through others unconditionally and continuously.

Change your habits and outlook and you'll change the world...

~ The surest way to improve life around you is to make lasting improvements in your habits and outlook that will focus you on serving the bigger ONE through adding the highest value in all situations.

The messenger pointing to the path is not the path itself...

~ All our spiritual gurus, avatars, saints, prophets, and even those we call gods incarnate are only messengers pointing to a path that helps us unveil the Divine residing within all of us.

We will be completely misdirected and deluded if, instead of following the path, we begin worshiping the messenger.

The promises you keep are not just an obligation, but reflect your integrity...

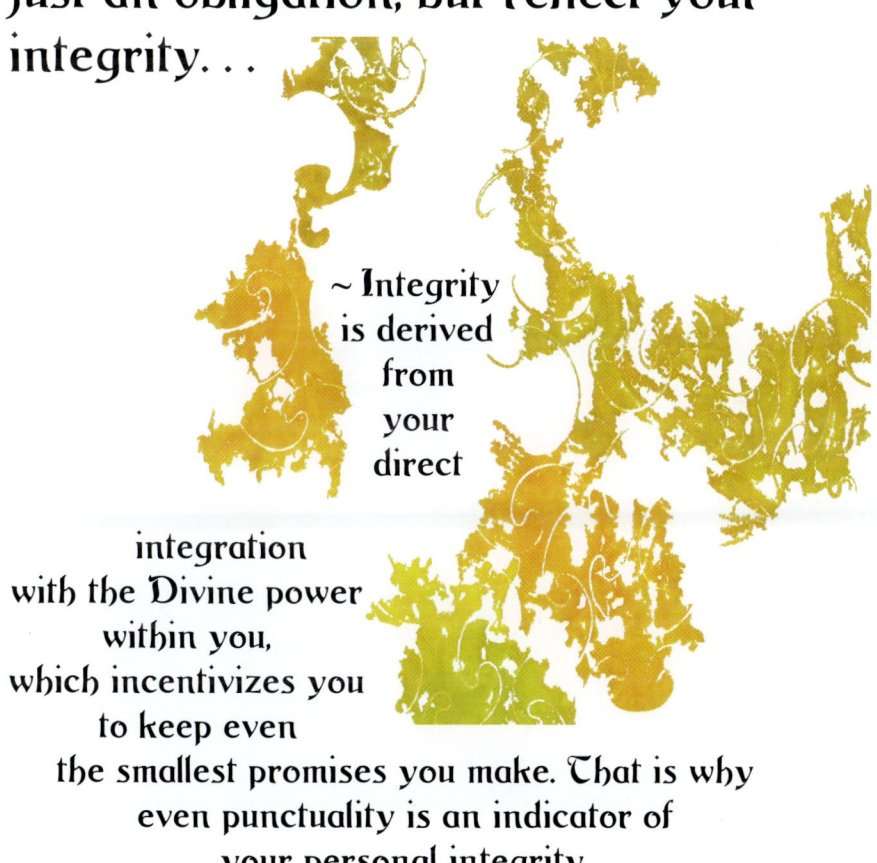

~ Integrity is derived from your direct integration with the Divine power within you, which incentivizes you to keep even the smallest promises you make. That is why even punctuality is an indicator of your personal integrity.

It is the Divine power within us that empowers us to be a true leader...

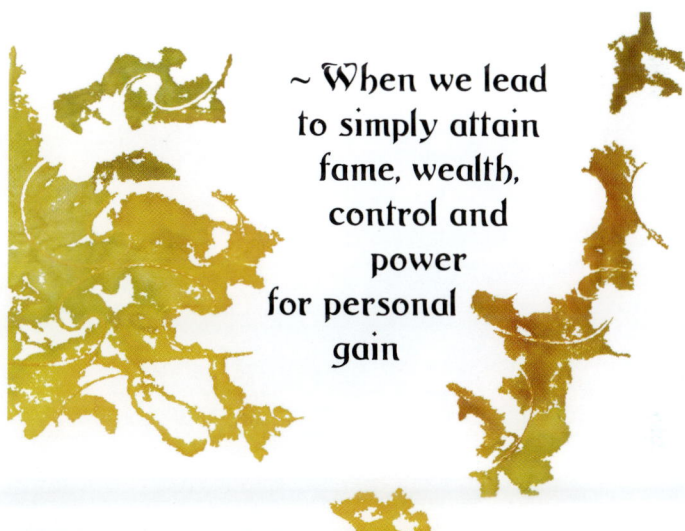

~ When we lead to simply attain fame, wealth, control and power for personal gain we disconnect from the universal Divine force within us. It is only when we engage in a cause that makes a difference unconditionally to those around us that we invoke the Divine power within us and its resources and become a true leader.

You are either a boss or a slave...

~ It all depends on what in you is leading and who in you is being led.

If you are led by your five senses, insecurities, fear, and greed — your quintessential ego — then you are a slave, not a boss. But if you are led by the real you, the Divine power and keeping your five senses disciplined to serve the bigger ONE, then you are a boss.

Until quality becomes your conscience,
it will slip through your fingers every time...

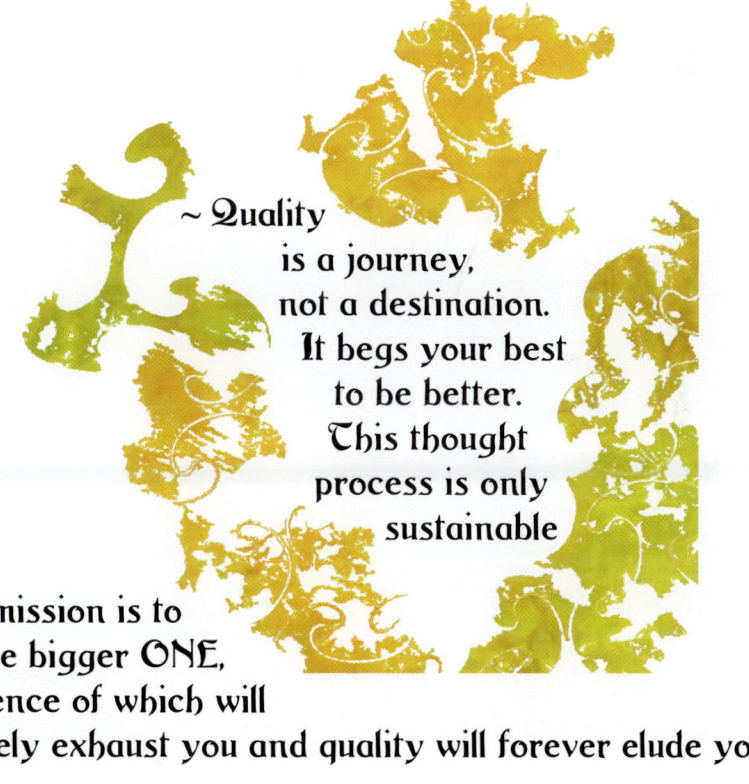

~ Quality is a journey, not a destination. It begs your best to be better. This thought process is only sustainable if your mission is to serve the bigger ONE, the absence of which will completely exhaust you and quality will forever elude you.

To succeed, you must find your passion...

~ If you look for passion in a subject, skill, experience, obsession or in a mentor, you'll be greatly deceived and disappointed. We come with passion already planted in our true selves. All we need to do to discover our passion is to discover our true selves, which will make us passionate about practicing excellence not mediocrity in every thought and action.

Creativity is elevated to the highest plateau when we — our egos — get out of its way...

~ Our ego creates duality, the illusion of us versus them, and we lose our connection to the divinity within us. Since all our creativity is gifted by the Divine, the presence of ego not only inhibits our creativity, but fills us with insecurity, thereby putting us in a highly stress-filled mode.

There is no difference between a business contract and conditional love...

~ Love is only truly love when it is unconditional. When there are conditions, it is only a lopsided, one-way business arrangement, which will instead of healing and empowering you, deplete you, derail you, and fill you with stress.

Your peace, harmony, and success are directly tied to the promises you keep...

~ In the Oneness paradigm, all your promises are in essence made to the bigger ONE, the Divine within all of us. If you cannot deliver on your promises, you are literally cheating the Divine within everyone.

Don't look for balance in life, look for harmony...

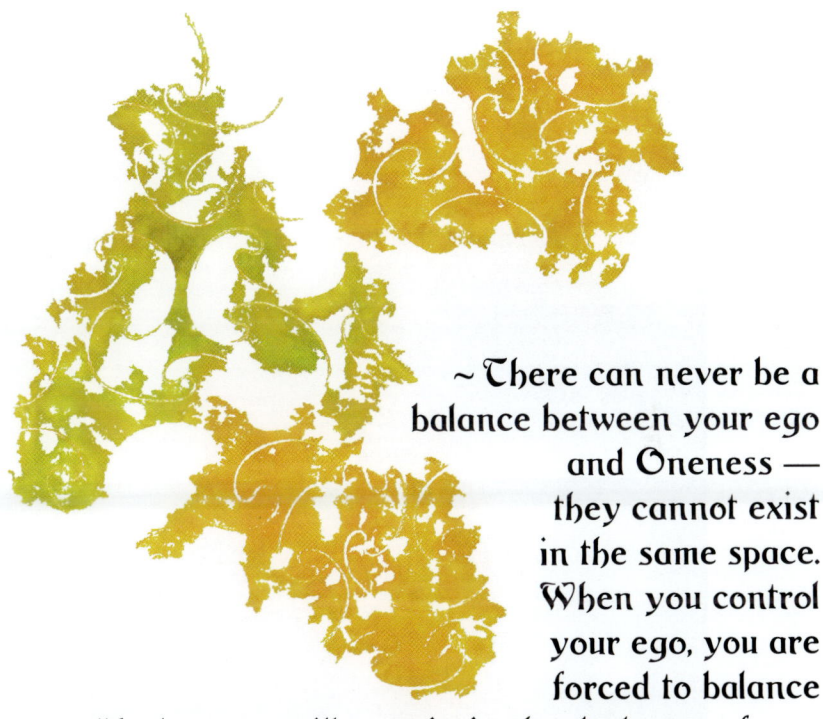

~ There can never be a balance between your ego and Oneness — they cannot exist in the same space. When you control your ego, you are forced to balance your life, but you still remain in the darkness of ego. It is only when you bring the light of Oneness, ego disappears and harmony prevails.

True joy comes from focusing on the journey of life rather than the destination...

~ Destinations are always tied to expectation, which brings anxiety and stress. Journeys bring joy as they are tied to exploration and discovery, which inspire gratefulness and acceptance of whatever comes.

If we put all of our focus on each step of our journey, the destination will take care of itself.

Ego is an illusion — true reality is Oneness...

~ Small ego or big ego or even humility is in fact part of the same confusion as they are merely an illusion originating from our mistaken sense of identity. Until we unveil our true identity — that of Oneness — we will be forever lost in the falsehood of our illusionary egos.

Success is tied to excellence and failure to mediocrity...

~ Until we engage our "true self" in doing a task, the outcome will remain mediocre at best. Our true self — an integral part of the Divine force — produces excellence through continuously bettering its best.

However, it only gives its blessing and support when we engage in projects that unconditionally add value and make a difference to the bigger One.

In the Oneness paradigm, forgiveness is irrelevant...

~ Forgiveness becomes an issue when we segregate ourselves from one another and thus it comes from our egos.

However, any wrong doing will generate pain the same way as when the hammer in your right hand hits the thumb of your left hand. If you can't feel the pain and suffering of others, you are still disconnected and not operating in the Oneness paradigm.

Kindness is weakness when fueled by pity...

~ Pity is part of egoic thinking wherein we feel superior to someone else.

Kindness is the result of the miraculous collaboration of a pure heart and clean mind. For kindness to become your strength, it must be a state of being inspired by your complete immersion in Oneness.

Love of God cannot be understood and therefore practiced until we comprehend God's existence in every living being. . .

~ If we disrespect, cheat, and lie to our fellow human beings and sit in our little prayer rooms reciting God's name over and over, this is all in vain and we are grossly misleading ourselves. It is only through the paradigm of Oneness that we can remember, pray, touch, and love God.

The underlying force moving us toward non-violence is experiencing and actually feeling others' pains...

~ Once we can feel others' pain, there is no way we can practice violence. However, to experience others' pain, we must operate in the Oneness paradigm at all times. When we see the presence of the same Divine in everyone, how can we even think of harming or even saying anything rude to others.

All of our conventional methods of seeking God are flawed...

~ Prayer, meditation, seeking blessings, petitioning, selfless doing and even gratefulness are contaminated by our egos, which make us operate in duality.

In the purest form of Oneness, we simply do not exist and thus cannot conduct any of these activities as we are completely dissolved in the Divine. Hence, there is no separation and nothing to seek.

All our creativity, good thoughts, and deeds come from the Divine wisdom within us...

~ If we take the credit, we endorse egoic thinking, which segregates us from unifying Oneness. To stay in Oneness, we must give credit to the Divine through its outlets, such as our colleagues and associates. That is why taking credit for work merely gives you a seat on the team.
    Giving credit to others
        makes you a leader.

Until you can experience God in all...

...you can't experience God at all.

101 Gems for Re-Aligning Your Life

Living in the present anchored in Oneness gives you a fresh start...

...as you let go of the unproductive baggage of old failures, stale issues, and uncertainties for the future.

Freedom is the most misunderstood concept in light of everything being guided and controlled by the unbending and unchanging laws of the universe...

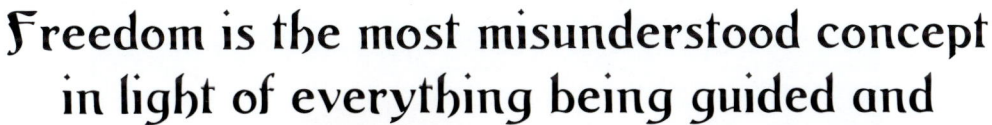

~ Therefore, the only true freedom we have is to choose and live our disciplines that are in full compliance with these laws.

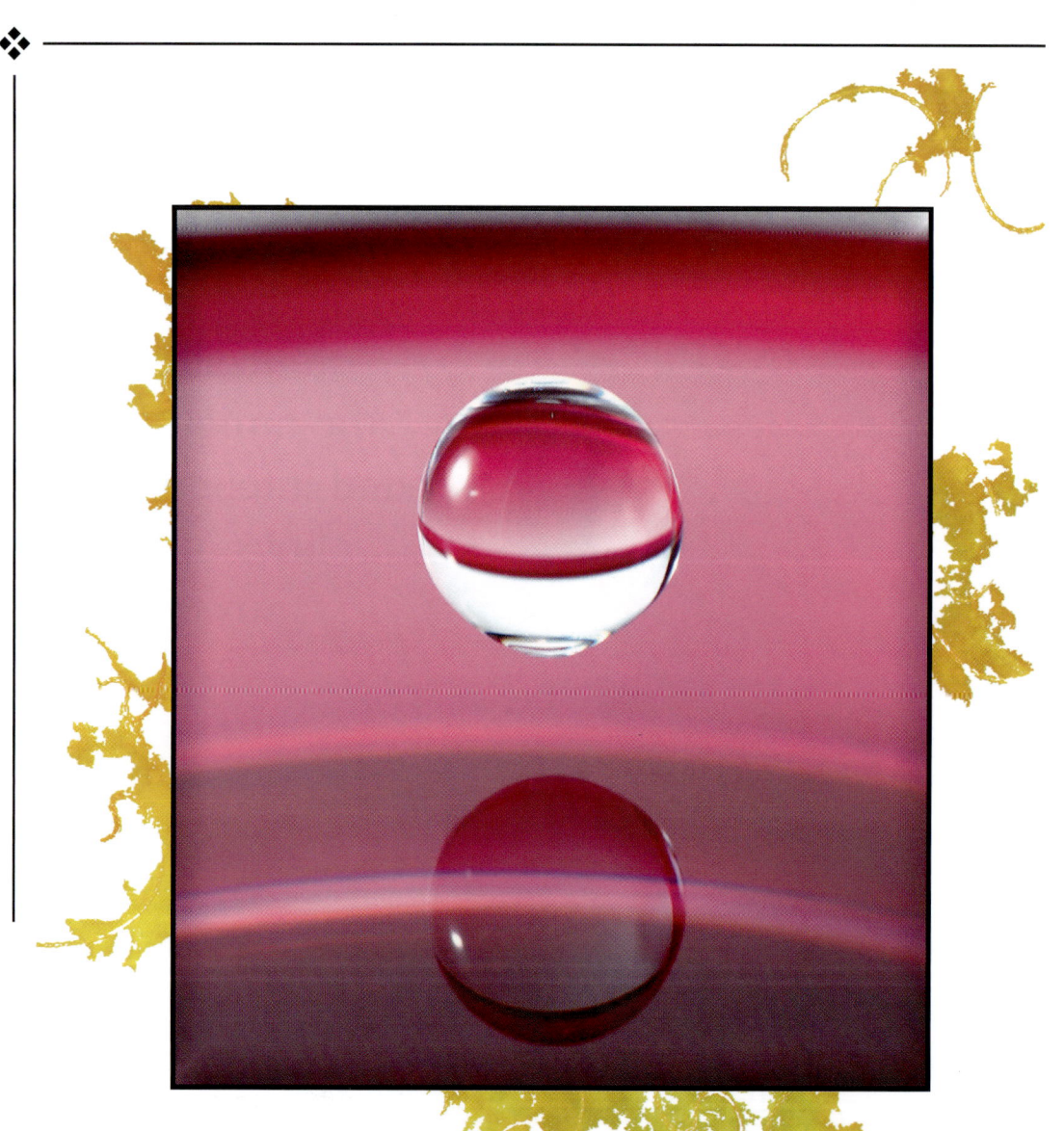

There is no better and more powerful motivator than the spiritual inspiration and empowerment that comes from operating in the

Oneness paradigm...

~ All boredom, discouragement, insecurity, and defeat are merely the absence of Oneness.

Unconditional loving, giving, and serving is a mindset that originates with the absence of your ego...

~ and is supported by experiencing the presence of the Divine force within you.

101 Gems for Re-Aligning Your Life

Most complex problems very often have a simple solution...

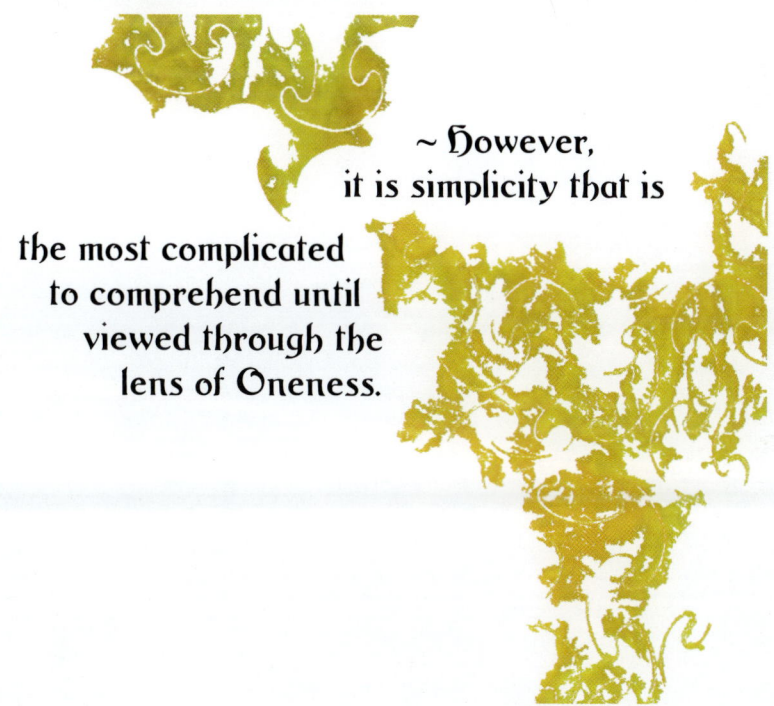

~ However, it is simplicity that is the most complicated to comprehend until viewed through the lens of Oneness.

Our success should never be measured against others, or our awards and possessions...

~ It is instead a measure of our innate capability and uninhibited capacity to serve Oneness unconditionally — in everyone around us — by constantly improving our personal best.

What we say always reflects our state of being...

~ When we are infected with insecurities, ego and fear, we speak a polluted language and our spoken words lack clarity and impact. The true depth, meaning, and power of our messages only comes through when we are completely integrated in Oneness and thus free of all these infections and agendas.

Often, freedom of speech takes away our freedom and enslaves us...

~ In the Oneness paradigm, we only have freedom of speech when our spoken words are void of our egos and instead add value and make a difference. Always remember that we become a slave of the words we have spoken and master of the ones we have not.

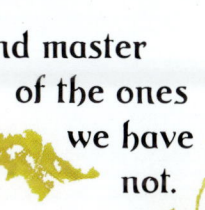

The past is history, the future merely a dream…

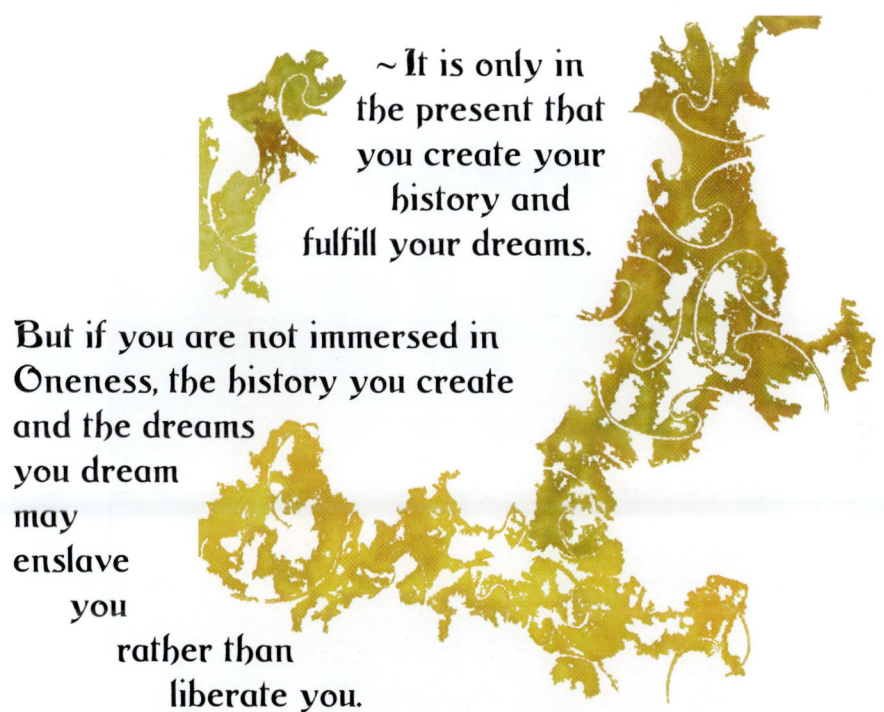

~ It is only in the present that you create your history and fulfill your dreams.

But if you are not immersed in Oneness, the history you create and the dreams you dream may enslave you rather than liberate you.

101 Gems for Re-Aligning Your Life

The language spoken by your values and actions is far more impactful than the language you express through words...

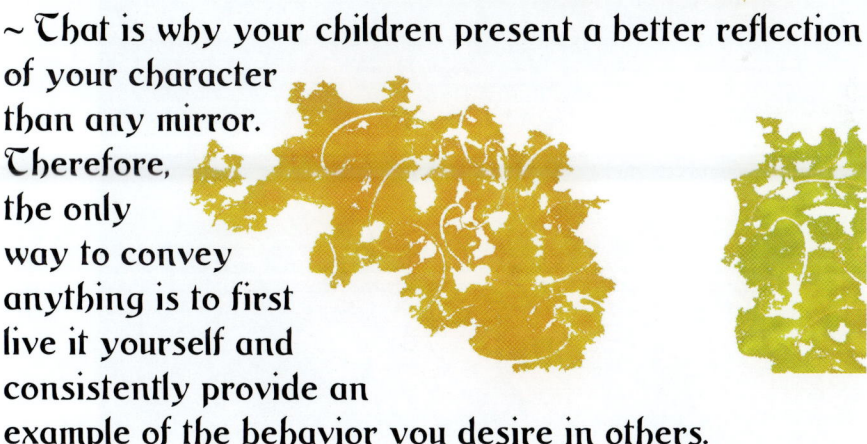

~ That is why your children present a better reflection of your character than any mirror. Therefore, the only way to convey anything is to first live it yourself and consistently provide an example of the behavior you desire in others.

Our human body has a short lifespan, but the Divine power that enlivens us does not...

~ Let the Divine
in you make all of your
decisions — as it lives
forever and will be
able to meet
the test of time —

in order to eliminate
the possibility of making
short-term, erroneous decisions.
Simultaneously, in utter gratefulness, attend to your
responsibilities and live your life as if it is
your last day to live.

No matter how we arrange or build
or decorate our lives,
they remain imperfect...

~ At best, it will be a compromise until we unveil the uncompromising and perfect Divinity residing within all of us.

Automatically,
our life falls perfectly
into place once we keep
our focus on unconditionally
loving and serving
this omnipresent Divinity.

Just having the knowledge of "the Divine force living within you"
will not transform you...

~ Knowledge alone

never does.

It is living that knowledge that will transform you. Until you begin to live Oneness and experience the Divine power within everyone — and all your decisions and actions reflect that unconditionally — this empowering transformation is not possible.

Without the light of Oneness, we will always remain in the darkness of ignorance...

~ It takes an incredible amount of knowledge, experience, intelligence, courage, and a herculean effort to reveal the true extent of our ignorance. But it will only take a split second of empowering Oneness to enlighten us and free us from the shackles of ignorance.

Just as you can't experience the fragrance of the most beautiful perfume when it's been added to a bottle that has garlic in it, similarly, you simply can't practice Oneness until you remove your own "garlic"...

~ Therefore, the first step towards practicing Oneness is self-purification through unconditional acceptance and gratefulness, which will keep you in the present and block all contaminations from entering.

Discipline only empowers you when you distinctly understand "who" in you is imposing the discipline for the "what" in you...

~ Your ability to say no to yourself — your self-indulgent five senses and forever starving ego —

leads to self-empowerment that brings you true and sustainable self-respect and confidence.

It is foolhardy to think that we can own either fire or money...

~ Fire and money are gifted to us by the bigger ONE, but are merely tools depending on how we use them. When our egos, fears, greed, and self-serving agendas are running the show, fire and money will destroy us.
When we are operating in the ego-free Oneness paradigm, the same fire and money will protect us.

Your greatest asset is at the same time housed within your own biggest obstacle...

~ Your biggest asset is the Divine power housed within your biggest obstacle, your human body, which is enslaved by your ego, insecurities, greed, selfish agendas, and your short-lived indulgences. With insight, an ordinary mirror can expose both at a glance.

Clarity of purpose, not willpower, motivates and sustains you to practice self-discipline...

~ It is the wisdom of Oneness that gives you a clear mission and true purpose in life. This clarity of purpose eventually brings you success and happiness through selflessly and unconditionally adding the highest value.
It is only at this point that you are truly motivated to practice and live your personal disciplines.

Simplicity without grace is merely laziness disguised...

...which only leads to mediocrity.

Respect is the super glue that holds all relationships together...

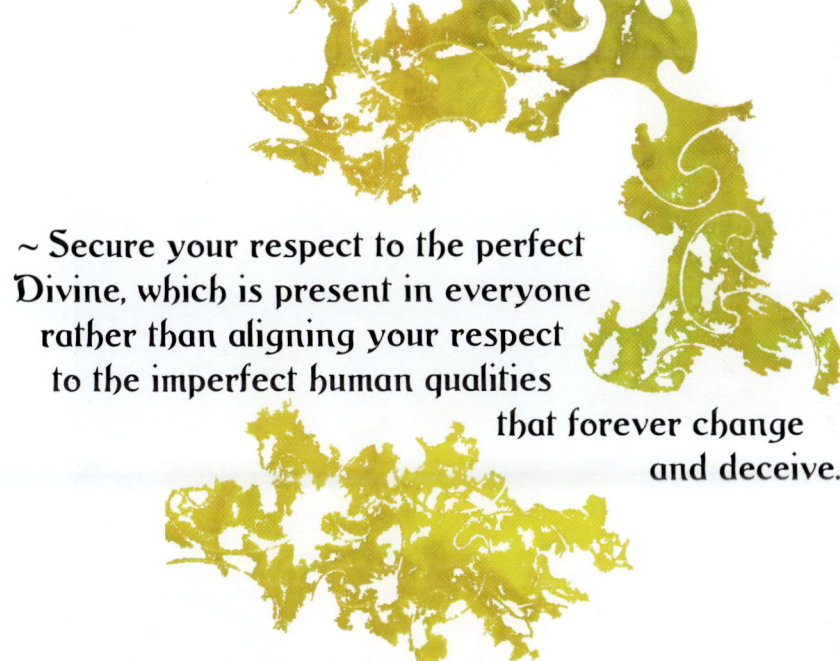

~ Secure your respect to the perfect Divine, which is present in everyone rather than aligning your respect to the imperfect human qualities that forever change and deceive.

Respect is unsustainable when it comes from worldly accolades such as success, wealth, title, talents, education, and any other worldly accomplishments...

~ It is only sustainable when it is tied to the flawless Divinity present in all of us.

True confidence...

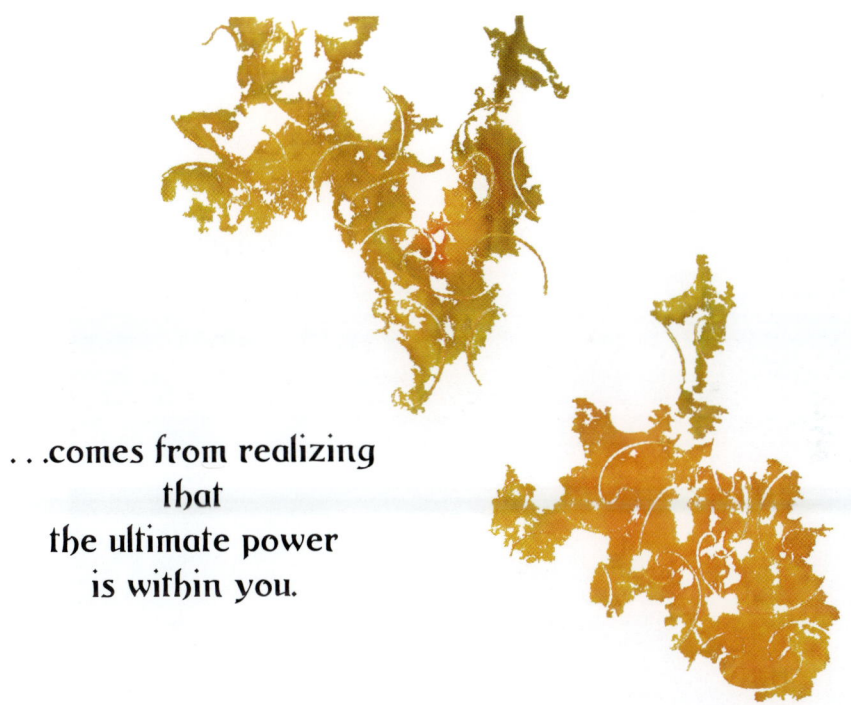

...comes from realizing
that
the ultimate power
is within you.

True love...

...is the art of complete surrender
of our ego and selfish agendas
to the bigger
ONE.

True friendship...

...is the art of being

a friend rather than accumulating friends.

The true power of a message...

...comes from living
the message
rather than delivering it.

True, uncompromising success...

...is the art of never accepting mediocrity or failure.

Unconditional gratefulness is the most empowering mindset...

...as it leaves no room for complaints, negativity, self-pity, and all self-inflicted miseries.

Before you can conquer anything...

...you have to conquer yourself — and before you can conquer yourself, you have to know who you are.

To find who you truly are, look deeply into your eyes in a mirror and witness the Divine Force within you, the real you...

~ Caution: This awareness will quickly be overwhelmed and negated by ego, insecurity, fear, and greed. Therefore, choose to continuously and unconditionally live and express the presence of this Divinity within yourself and everyone you come across.

When you focus on removing your contaminations — prejudice, fear, greed, indulgences,

and all ego-driven agendas...

...you won't have to seek God. God will come through you naturally and effortlessly.

Ego divides...

...selflessness unites.

Most of the time, the secret of happiness lies not in finding the right answers...

...but in unveiling the right questions.

The moment you feel you understand everything...

...be assured you understand nothing.

Our capacity to express uninhibited gratefulness...

...reflects the extent of our selflessness.

The best way to get out of depression…

…is to undertake projects —
unconditionally
and without
reservation —
that add value
to everyone
and everything
around you.

The primary goal of life is to break the cycle of birth & death...

~ We are in this cycle to resolve the karma we create, both good and bad. To break this cycle, we must detach from both karmas and see the real doer behind everything — the Divine — at which time we become merely a witness, not the doer. When this happens, we become a conduit for the Divine and become pure goodness rather than just doing good deeds.

Life is a journey, not a destination...

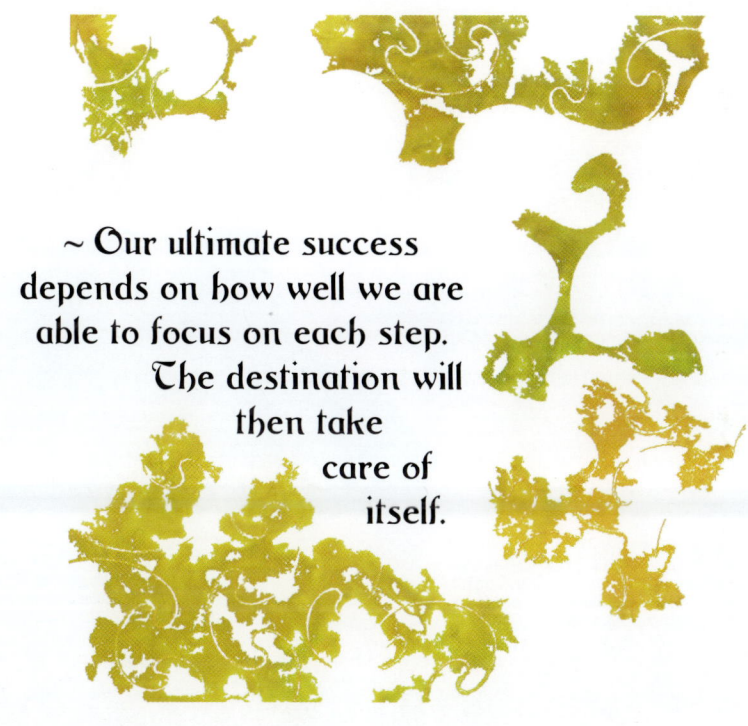

~ Our ultimate success depends on how well we are able to focus on each step. The destination will then take care of itself.

True education is the art...

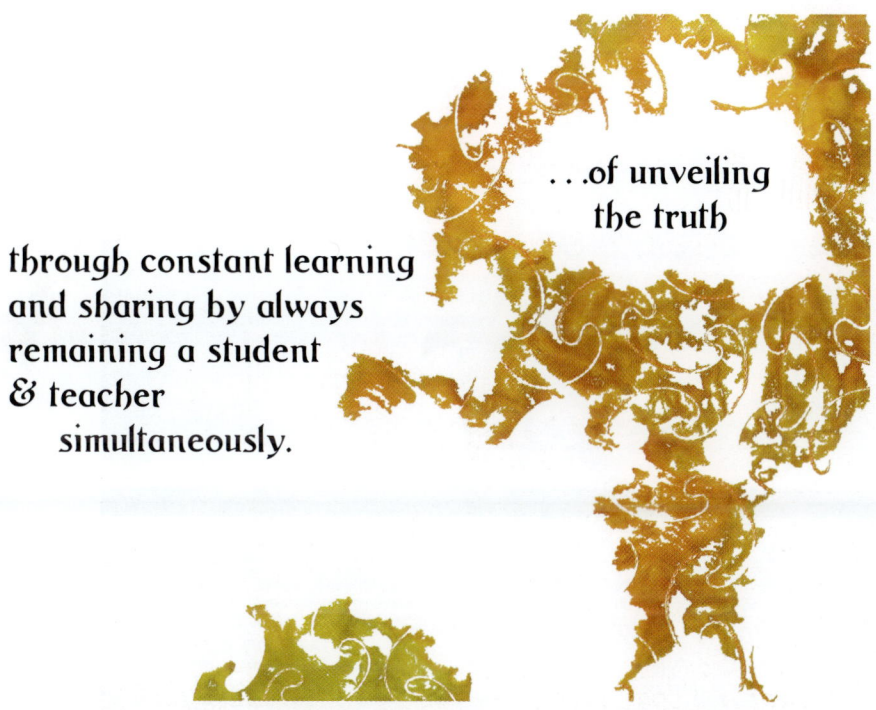

...of unveiling the truth

through constant learning and sharing by always remaining a student & teacher simultaneously.

Unconditional loving, serving, and giving...

...cannot happen until we get out of the way.

People who see difficulties and obstacles as opportunities to serve and add the highest value...

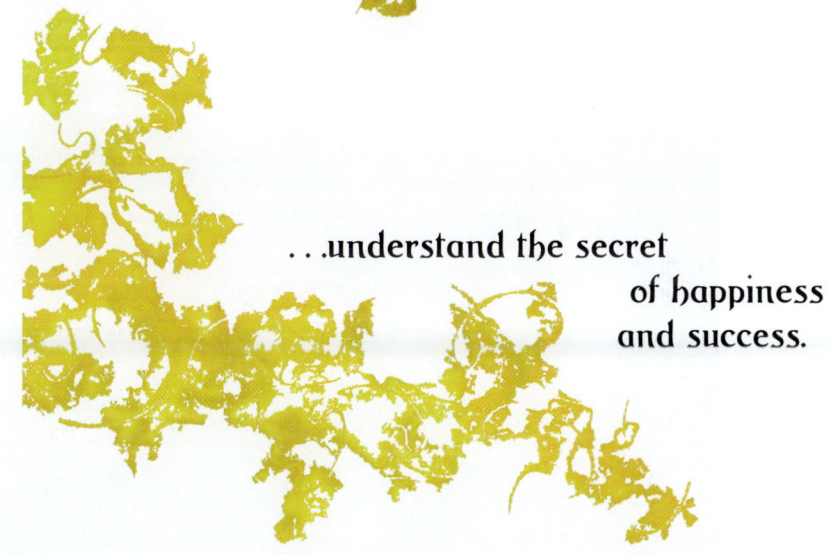

...understand the secret of happiness and success.

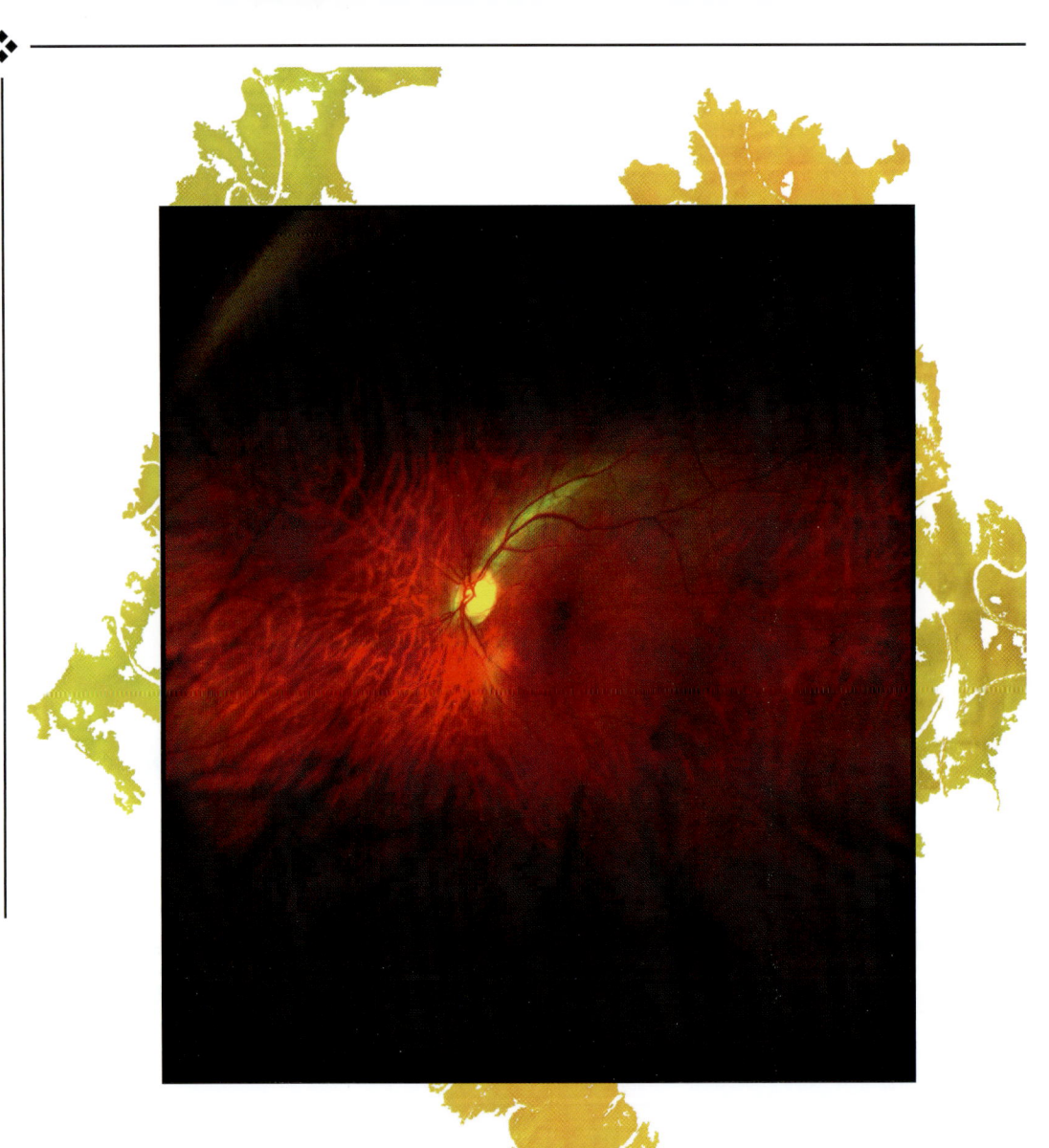

Often, our minds segregate us...

...because all of the experiences gathered by our minds are incomplete and erroneous. Whereas our heart unites us as it is directly connected to the bigger ONE.

Once you begin to operate in Oneness...

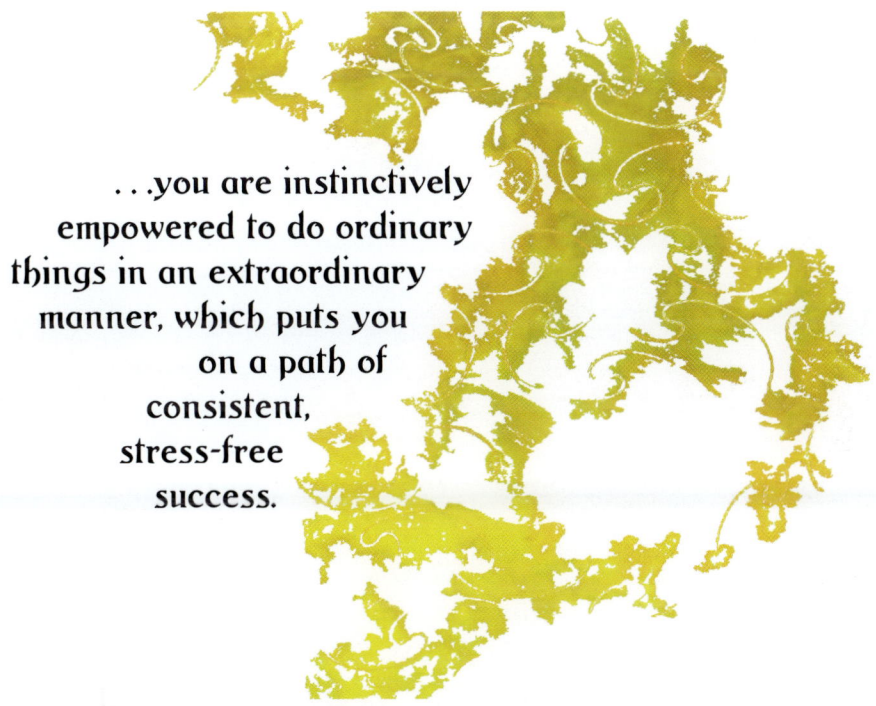

...you are instinctively empowered to do ordinary things in an extraordinary manner, which puts you on a path of consistent, stress-free success.

Table of Photographers

Photos courtesy of Thinkstockphotos.com and David Christel

Andrew_Mayovskyy	2
David Christel	4
kojihirano	6
Tippapatt	8
mycola	10
TomasSereda	12
Ryhor Bruyeu	14
B_Miller	16
CarolinaBirdman	18
TothGaborGyula	20
tvphoto	22
David Christel	24
losw	26
Vladimir Melnik	28
Kseniya Abramova	30
KerstinIvarsson	32
Minerva Studio	34
Игорь Гончаренко Igor Goncharenko	36
vencavolrab	38

silverjohn	40
Liquidlibrary	42
Richard Valdez	44
David Christel	46
Fuse	48
Design Pics/Carl Shaneff	50
Biletskiy_Evgeniy	52
Top Photo Group	54
RyanKing999	56
DawidKasza	58
yangphoto	60
Eric Gevaert	62
OST	64
dreamnikon	66
Anna Kucherova	68
CathyKeifer	70
PCHT	72
SergeyTimofeev	74
bestdesigns	76
MarkMirror	78
Daniela Pelazza	80
Fuse	82
Henk Bentlage	84
Mike_Pellinni	86
Auxins	88
Hannu Viitanen	90

Nick Biemans	92
Fuse	94
AndreAnita	96
Jupiterimages	98
Robert Babczynski	100
Artur Synenko	102
Anolis01	104
Fotomicar	106
agustavop	108
nattanan726	110
Andrew_Mayovskyy	112
defun	114
johnnya123	116
KhonMaerim	118
TongRo Images	120
Zoonar RF	122
silverjohn	124
Anup Shah	126
Mike_Pellinni	128
Anton_Petrus	130
photo_grafix	132
Art Wolfe	134
Davesangster	136
Yuriy_Kulik	138
aniszewski	140

HenriVdl	142
andreusK	144
topdeq	146
Serjio74	148
huad262	150
Jane Tyson	152
David Christel	154
Herianus	156
Yana_N	158
Alan Dearing	160
Ivkovich	162
sborisov	164
VLukas	166
CarolinaBirdman	168
hisartwork	170
Toltek	172
IndrekV	174
StevanZZ	176
Serg_Velusceac	178
Fuse	180
Dendron	182
Marco Crisari	184
leightrail	186
David Christel	188
David Butler	190
egal	192

Ingram Publishing 194
Ig0rZh 196
moodboard 198
David Christel 200
Kostyantyn Schastnyy 202

Other Books by Ratanjit

How Oneness Changes Everything
Empowering Business Through 9 Universal Laws

TEA: The Recipe for Stress-Free Living

The Secret of Our Ultimate Success

Audios & Videos

The 9 Universal Laws of Success

The 25 Habits for Success

About the Author

Ratanjit Singh Sondhe emigrated from India to the United States in 1968 with no more than a few dollars in his pocket and the belief that our purpose in life is to add value to the lives of those around us. Over the past 40 years, this purpose has brought Ratanjit great success. He was the founder and CEO of the international materials science company POLY-CARB, Inc., which was acquired by The DOW Chemical Company in 2007. He is the author of **How Oneness Changes Everything: Empowering Business Through 9 Universal Laws**. Ratanjit is also an educator, lecturer, author, radio & television host, well-respected member of the community, father, and a husband.

To help others achieve stress-free success and true joy, Ratanjit wrote **TEA: The Recipe for Stress-Free Living** and numerous award-winning papers, has hosted over 600 international radio and television programs, and has travelled the world delivering captivating words of wisdom to help others succeed, realize their true freedom, maximize their potential, take full control of their lives, unveil their true passion, and live stress-free. More information about Ratanjit S. Sondhe can be found online at www.ratanjit.com and www.discoverhelp.com.